"To speak of Nathan Jirovec is to speak of the goodness of our great God. Nathan's life has been a constant reminder of God's abundant mercy and grace. Watching God's hand on Nathan through the years has been a testament to *His* miraculous works as well as the balm of healing, for the hearts of the Jirovec family. Nathan's spirit of determination, and the steadfastness of the entire family in any situation that arises, has always been their song through the years, giving glory only to God. They have seen first hand, God turn tragedy into triumph, insurmountable grief into gladness, and struggles into strength. In *Finding Nathan* we have found not Nathan's story, but God's story and the treasure of the everlasting faithfulness of our Father. It has been my utmost privilege to know the Jirovecs and be counted as family. God is so good!"

— Rosa McCandless

"Nathan's life and story are nothing short of miraculous. God's loving, guiding hand was present in his family's life well before this tragic accident, and therefore we have seen a wondrous story unfold of beauty for ashes. From a robust little five-year-old boy to the Godly young man he is today, Nathan and his family have claimed God's faithfulness and His plan for their lives. Because of this, the tragedy that occurred on a cold night in December 1995 did not destroy them but became a story of inspiration for all who hear it. Under the direst circumstances, Nathan never quit. When someone says, "I can't do it", our first thoughts go to Nathan and how he has overcome more than most people can even fathom. Countless times, we have told his story, and his story has inspired others. We are sure his story will inspire you as well."

— Steve & Shelly Lake

"Nathan's story reminds us that life is full of the unexpected. Pain and grief and storms come our way. But Nathan's attitude reminds us of more. Much more. He has chosen to live a life of hope and joy. We can find those ingredients throughout his story. I'm honored to consider him my friend. Read his story and you'll feel like Nathan's friend also."

— Chris Maxwell
Author, Speaker, Spiritual Director

FINDING NATHAN

ONE FAMILY'S STORY OF RISING FROM TRAGEDY TO GRACE

NATHAN JIROVEC
WITH CHRIS MAXWELL

FINDING NATHAN
One Family's Story of Rising from Tragedy to Grace

Cover and Interior Page design by True Potential, Inc.

ISBN: 978-1-943852-76-5 (paperback)
ISBN: 978-1-943852-77-2 (e-book)
Library of Congress Control Number: 2017964212

True Potential, Inc.
PO Box 904, Travelers Rest, SC 29690
www.truepotentialmedia.com

Printed in the United States of America.

To my mother, Shirley Jirovec.

This book will be a remembrance of the lows and highs we experienced and overcame together as a family.

I love you, Mom, and always will.

Thank you for all you have done in my life. I know now, it was not easy for you when I was small, losing a son and then having to take care of me.

In spite of the spiritual and physical pain you went through, you just kept on believing and trusting in our God; putting one foot in front of the other and kept on moving. Thank you for not quitting on me when I needed you most. You mean more to me than you could know.

The countless hours spent taking me to therapy and to the hospitals, practicing patterning and making me crawl. I know I was hard to push through day after day of exercises and therapy.

When others ask, "How did you make it so far?"

I tell them that can it is because of my Mom. She wanted a better life for me … a normal life.

When hard times come, you plow straight through and help those along the way. Much of what motivates me, moves me, and determines my decisions comes from your commitment and example.

You are the Virtuous Woman that Proverbs speaks of.

Mom, you are the reason I am succeeding in life today.

I love you deeply Mama.

Your Little Boy,
Nathan

Contents

Foreword

I have known Nathan Jirovec pretty much since his birth. From the very beginning of his life and at every stage thereof I have seen some common and dominant character traits. The greatest character trait I observed was his love for God and desire to please Him. That is why at the age of 5 he announced he wanted to be a missionary! I have fond memories of playing hide and seek with him and his other brothers at family get-togethers. He had a tenacity wrapped in kindness in all of his competitive play. He was never ambitious at the expense of another, and at a time or two, I even saw him sacrifice his own potential to save another's.

These traits have buoyed to him as he struggled through the difficulty of surviving a tragic accident that took his brother's life and almost took his own. He persevered when others thought he was someone else, but he could not communicate. He fought to regain as much use of his body when nature was following a different course. He fought gallantly and has been a victor in more battles in his first 20 years than most people fight in a lifetime!

Nathan is an inspiration to all who have a sound mind and know him. I believe you will receive untold blessings from reading the story of his life; and therefore, I highly recommend this book to all readers of any age. May his character, his fighting spirit, and his kindness jump off the pages of this book into your heart as you read and put yourself into his shoes.

Pastor Tim Coleman,
Nathan's "Uncle Tim"
35th Avenue Baptist Church, Phoenix, Arizona

Preface

I first met Randy Jirovec, Nathan's dad, over the phone in August of 2014. He told me that Nathan had a story he wanted to share in a book. Then he mailed me a rather substantial package of files, interview recordings, images, medical records, pages from a journal, news clippings and mortuary bulletins.

As a publisher, I'm accustomed to reading my authors' stories from their submitted manuscripts. But this time, instead of a well organized Word® document on my screen, I was facing a stack of papers and other artifacts of data collected over more than twenty years. After sorting through the stack, listening to recordings, reading through personal journals and hospital and emergency responder reports, and holding in my hands the mortuary service bulletins for two little boys, dated just weeks apart, I understood that this collection of pieces on my desk held Nathan's story. And not just Nathan's, but also his family's story, and, to some extent, the story of everyone Nathan's journey has touched.

I emailed Nathan, now a young man, and arranged a phone call. The Nathan I met on the phone was not the little boy from the story the medical records and journal entries told. This Nathan was a young man. He spoke in a polite, halting voice, always listening before commenting, always adding "sir." The Nathan I spoke with on the phone was someone who had overcome

PREFACE

great tragedy and much pain; someone who had rewritten the story of Nathan the stack of papers on my desk told. This Nathan had two stories, and it is only in both, I came to learn, that we can truly understand and appreciate the unique and inspiring young man Nathan is today.

A book is a container, and well made, it can tell a story. But Nathan's story has been housed in a collection of documents and bits of historical data, in old photos, journals, and tape recordings. Much of Nathan's story, I suspected, was also still carried in the memories Nathan and his family still held close. This story, to be shared with the world, would need to be extracted from all of these sources and crafted into a cohesive whole. Like refining silver from ore, someone with great skill as a writer, interviewer and listener would need to shape Nathan's story into the form of a book.

My friend and author Chris Maxwell has written and ghostwritten many books and hundreds of magazine articles and curriculums. Beyond his talent as an author, which is considerable, Chris is a listener, and he listens from his heart. Chris has spent months with Nathan's story and time with Nathan's family in Oregon. Chris, I believe, is a craftsman and has refined Nathan's story and shaped it into something that can be shared with the world in the form of a book.

Thank you, Chris, for your skill. And thank you, Nathan, for writing your story with your life and sharing it with the world.

My hope for you, dear reader, is to understand both stories in this book and come away with a life richer in hope, inspiration, optimism, and grit from *Finding Nathan*.

Steve Spillman,
Publisher

Appreciation

Thanks to those who helped during the writing and editing process: Aaron Westbury, Rebecca James, and Clarke Sowell.

Introduction: The Unexpected

The unexpected is inevitable.

Big or small, we are all caught off guard by the heartbreak and distress that this life brings. Whether it is being stood up by a close friend or the loss of a family member, life will continually knock us down. The important decision is that we get back up. It may seem as if I have endured more than the average person, but the fact of the matter is we all are subject to heartache, and we have all endured physical and emotional pain. Life is tricky and unpredictable; we shouldn't be surprised when something unexpected happens - even the unimaginable. No matter how hard we try to prepare, no matter how hard we try to be ready for the unexpected trials of life, we usually are not ready for the storms when they come.

We are rarely prepared.

Often, we start a normal day but end the day feeling completely overwhelmed.

During these tough hours, I learned that I could rely on my God. The Lord used the Scriptures to comfort my soul, and I don't even know how many times I thought of II Corinthians 12:9, "And he said unto me, My grace is sufficient for thee: for my strength is made perfect in weakness." As a Christian, I know that God does indeed supply every need and gives more than enough grace to get through any difficulty life hands me. I truly believe Isaiah 41:10 when it says, "Fear thou not; for I am with thee: be not dismayed for I am thy God: I will strengthen thee; yea, I will help thee; yea, I will uphold thee with the right hand of my righteousness."

During the times in life that we feel completely alone and are convinced that there is no one to lean on or talk to, we always have one person to whom we are able to turn when we experience unexpected heartaches: God. When things happen to us that make no sense to us, and when we have to endure through trials that we feel are unjust, there is always one person on whom we can depend. Because I have a personal relationship with Jesus Christ, I know that He is always there for me. I do not have to depend upon a mere human for comfort because I know that the Lord knows what I am going through. He can provide grace to get me through every trial, every heartache, and every unexpected tragedy that will ever happen to me. Not only can the Lord do this, but He will.

I steadfastly believe that God provides us with the strength to get through every trial and that God will provide enough grace to help us endure anything life can throw at us. Even though it may be difficult to accept the fact that everything happens to us for a reason, God is always in control, even when we don't understand.

FINDING NATHAN

I want to encourage you to keep pressing on. I am living with hope, and I want you to have hope too.

I have endured great tragedy. I currently live with both physical and mental disabilities, but I can still smile after all that I've been through, and I want you to keep smiling too. I am still looking forward to the blessings that lie ahead, and I want you to keep looking forward to the blessings that are to come in your own life.

I am disabled.

My life is tough.

Things are hard. But I understand the fact that other people have it harder than I have it.

Who has it harder, the man who is permanently disabled because of a car accident or the man who just unexpectedly lost a loved one? What's worse, to struggle every day of life with a physical disability, or to struggle with the trials, traumas, and hurts that life can bring to any of us? Do I understand every problem you face? I'm sure I don't. I don't even understand myself all the time.

However, I fully believe that my experiences allow me to relate to people who are experiencing unbelievable heartaches and tragedies. When others look at my life, I hope they think one thought: If this man can be happy, I can be happy too! If a man with multiple, permanent disabilities can make it, I can make it also.

Introduction

With God's help, you can be happy.

You can do more than just barely make it through life.

You can live on the winning side.

CHAPTER 1

Life as I Know It

People stare.

They wonder what happened.

Sometimes I go to a grocery store. People see me walking with a limp. They see me doing everything with my left arm because I can't use my right. The cashier talks to me when I check out, but it takes me a while to say what I want to say. At the grocery store, it takes me three times as long as someone else to buy the same shopping list that they may have. My mind works faster than my body.

Strangers, they are. If they only knew my story, they would know that I, Nathan Jirovec, am blessed. I, Nathan Jirovec, am saved by grace. In the words of former Major League Baseball player Lou Gehrig: "Today, I consider myself the luckiest man on the face of the Earth." Gehrig uttered these famous words shortly after he was diagnosed with ALS, otherwise known as "Lou Gehrig's disease."

Life as I Know It

Sometimes it takes a tragic event to realize how blessed we truly are. Sometimes it takes the loss of so much to realize how much it is that we still have. Sometimes we lose a grip on reality. When faced with adversity, things that may have seemed important become quite trivial, while things that were less important to us begin to mean so much more.

That is what happened to me.

It is through great tragedy that I am where I am today. Through great loss I am able to fully appreciate all that I do have.

If I had to fill the sentence "Nathan Jirovec is …," I could do so with many different terms. Of the many, college educated, financial investor, and successful entrepreneur can be applied. Along with these, the titles mentally disabled, physically disabled, and brain damaged can also be applied. These are titles that are very rarely intermingled. It is by God's amazing grace that I am here today.

I am here to tell my story. A story of unimaginable heartbreak and devastation. A story of tragic loss and incredible difficulty performing everyday tasks. But more than any of that, my story is a story of great hope.

I am writing because we all experience tragedy in our lives. When I look around, I don't think I have it worse than anyone else, but the suffering I deal with makes me want to reach out a helping hand to you. I want to say, "We are all rowing in the same boat on the same stormy waters. And, friend, I want to help you make it to the other side." One of the hardest parts of my journey is something that we all experience in life – the loss of a loved one. Whether it is losing a grandparent, mother or father, son or daughter, everyone will mourn the loss of a loved one at some point in his or her life. I just had to deal with it at a younger age than most.

Finding Nathan is about more than how I was found on a devastating evening in December. It is about more than the long-term effects of that disaster. It is about me and about my family. It is about you.

I had to find the Nathan that God created me to be. I had to find the Nathan God could use even when weaknesses are obvious to people who stare, to people who wonder what happened to me.

Finding Nathan is about me telling others what has really happened to me. And it is more than the eyes can see.

What happened?

I found myself. I found my potential and my purpose. I found new vision and new hope. I found life in the middle of what seemed like death.

So how did I get here?

LIFE AS I KNOW IT

How did I overcome the challenges that I have faced? How do I still overcome my weaknesses?

The answer is a simple one: It is only because of my Father in heaven. I remember when the doctors told me that I would never be like normal children. I remember when the specialists told me that I should come to grips with the fact that I would never enjoy all of life's most fascinating experiences. I remember when the people in the medical community warned me that I might never be able to accomplish the most simple, routine tasks of life. The fact of the matter is they are right - from a worldly perspective. But in the eyes of God, I can accomplish all that they told me that I cannot do. In fact, I can accomplish much more than what they told me I never would. I can, and have, accomplished things that people in the medical community cannot even begin to fathom. King Solomon was right when he said in Proverbs, "For a just man falleth seven times, and riseth up again" (Proverbs 24:16a, KJV).

Life as I know it isn't simple. But life, as you know, it isn't simple either. So, what should we do? Find ourselves. Find hope. And work to make our hopes realities.

From learning to tie my shoe with one hand, to learning to juggle the responsibilities of managing a successful business and maintaining good grades, I have learned to accomplish all that had once seemed impossible. I have learned that by taking one step at a time and refusing to give up, I can even twenty-two years later – as well as you and as anyone – endure anything.

CHAPTER 2

An Unforgettable Christmas Season

His name is Randy Jirovec.

He is my dad. He is the kindest, most loving person that I know.

Like a rock, he was there for me when I was too young to take care of myself. He was there during the dark days – when I was hanging between life and death.

He saw.

He knew.

He remembers.

I remember the days before the accident. My dad and I would go to church together. He and I, as well as my brothers Jonathan and Daniel, would leave hours early on the church bus. We would pick up all of those who wanted to attend but did not have a ride. The memories that we created on that bus will last a lifetime. They made us grow closer. It made me value my family above all else, and at the young age of five, those church trips instilled a faith that would be crucial for me to be able to face the adversity that I would soon be confronted with. Even to this day, my father means the world to me. Without him, I wouldn't be here.

I will forever be thankful for all that he has done in my life. Through bravery, he has made decisions that not only saved my life, but he has helped shape me into the man I am today.

If it wasn't for my faith, I don't know where I would be. If it wasn't for my father's faith, I don't know where I would be. It is by God's grace that I am alive, and the source of all my strength to never give up and to continue pushing on through all adversity rests solely in Jesus Christ alone. Fanny Crosby, the blind poet who gave us some of our best gospel lyrics, wrote:

Never be sad or desponding
Lean on the arm of thy Lord;
Dwell in the depths of His mercy,
Thou shalt receive thy reward.
Never give up! Never give up!
Never give up to thy sorrows,
Jesus will bid them depart.
Trust in the Lord! Trust in the Lord!
Sing when your trials are greatest,
Trust in the Lord and take heart!

Fanny Crosby was right. Never give up.

Finding Nathan

I have learned that by taking one step at a time and refusing to give up, anyone can endure anything. I have learned that you cannot fail as long as you are continually trying to accomplish your goals.

That's what I know, and that's what my dad knows, too.

They told me I would do things much slower than everyone else, but that didn't stop me from graduating high school – even if it took me longer to graduate. They told me that most people in my condition will be financially dependent upon someone else his entire life, but that didn't stop me from starting a successful business and enrolling in college. They didn't know how strong God can make a weak man. They didn't know how determined I could be. They didn't know how clever I could be.

Life came at me like a ton of bricks falling on an egg, but by God's grace, I didn't crack. I decided at a young age that I wasn't going to give up on living. I wouldn't let my disabilities hold me back from what God had planned for my life.

I believe that every child has that one adult family member in his or her life that they look forward to spending time with more than anyone else because he or she is able to hold on to his or her childlike demeanor.

For some children, it's a wild older cousin, a stepbrother, or even a gregarious grandparent.

An Unforgettable Christmas

For me, it was my crazy Uncle Rick. My brothers and I loved playing with Uncle Rick because, well, he was like us – a child at heart.

Christmas that year was supposed to be extra special because my Uncle Rick and his family were coming to Oregon to visit us during the Christmas season. My brothers and I loved spending time with my Uncle Rick, my Aunt Dawn and cousin Rachel. We especially loved playing with Uncle Rick because he would always find ways to make us laugh – he'd make goofy faces and talk in funny voices, the ultimate source of entertainment for a five year old – he would also wrestle with us, show us all sorts of neat tricks he knew, and play all sorts of games with us.

They lived in North Carolina, so it wasn't often that we had the opportunity to spend time with them.

While my uncle and his family were visiting us, we really enjoyed having time off to spend with our family during the Christmas season. When we weren't playing with Uncle Rick, my dad made us do things as a family. I remember one day, both my family and my uncle's family went up on the ridge behind our house to take a family picture. In the Jirovec household, taking a family photo was always an event – especially when you add in my crazy Uncle Rick and his family. We were having so much fun, it was hard to stop. I remember my parents trying to get us to stand still long enough for of us to be in position and smiling in unison to take the photo.

But despite the chaos, that moment will be one that I cherish for the rest of my life.

Little did I know that that was going to be the last picture taken of our entire family together. That photo has become very dear to me because it is the last photo I have of our entire family.

That night, the day before my accident, my family and I went to the mall to do some window-shopping and enjoy each other's company. We did not get to go to the mall very often, so it was a special treat for the family to do so.

The mall was perfect.

I could feel the Christmas atmosphere.

Things were peaceful.

All was calm.

The comfort and warmth of knowing that I was surrounded by my entire family produced within me a feeling of sweet serenity. Most people who go to a mall find joy in purchasing expensive items, but that is not why we were there. We were not interested in buying over-priced clothes, video games, or any other item that we didn't need. We were there to spend time as a family. Every item in every store in that mall could not add up to the value of being with my family on that marvelous night.

An Unforgettable Christmas

Everything was absolutely perfect.

Then suddenly, that peaceful feeling was ripped away.

"Jonathan! Jonathan!" I heard my dad call. "Jonathan, where did you go?!?"

My brother, Jonathan, had disappeared from the group. Trying to find a small child in an overcrowded mall is like trying to find a needle in a haystack. I could see the fear in my dad's eyes. This is every parent's worst nightmare – losing a child. In this case, the literal sense of the word "lost."

We started retracing our steps to locate Jonathan. After just a few minutes – that seemed like an eternity - my father saw Jonathan in the crowd, looking for us.

You could see the relief that swept across my father once he had found Jonathan, and the relief on Jonathan's face. After my father admonished Jonathan to stay with the family so he would not get lost or kidnapped, we continued through the mall.

I remember feeling so relieved that my brother had not been lost.

But little did I know that the feelings of fear and apprehension that my father and I felt over losing Jonathan in the mall would seem so insignificant just twenty-four hours later.

CHAPTER 3

The Wreck

It has now been over two decades since that dreadful day.

But somehow the memories of what happened are as vivid as if it had happened yesterday.

During the Christmas season of 1995, our lives were typical in every way. Everyone was a bit happier than usual. The spirit of Christmas filled the air, and we were all looking forward to every part of the holiday season – the family time, the special meals, the gift exchange, and the change of schedule.

Then came December 22.

It started out like every other day that winter: joyful.

My Uncle Rick was there making everyone laugh. My mother made a hot, delicious breakfast with all of my favorites. My dad, my brothers, and I were excited about the Christmas play that was set to take place that night. Everyone in my family had a role in the play.

The Wreck

My dad was part of a church bus team, helping pick up those who wanted to attend the Christmas play but did not have a ride. My mom was part of the production team to make sure the play went off without a hitch, and my brothers and I were playing various parts. We all had some responsibility connected with the play, so we had to make sure that we were at the church a few minutes early.

My parents wanted to make sure that they got all of us to the church on time. That responsibility mostly fell upon my mother since my dad had to leave the house early to meet the bus.

Normally, every time my dad was on the church bus, my brothers and I wanted to go along with him. We loved riding around in such a big bus, and I think that my dad enjoyed having us along for the ride. However, because my uncle and his family were going to stay home and come to the church with my mom, my brother Jonathan and I decided to stay home and play with Uncle Rick. My dad loved having all three of us with him on the bus, but Jonathan and I wanted to stay – we figured he could use that time to have father-son moments with my other brother, Daniel.

After a wonderful time together as a family that morning, my dad had to leave to meet the bus and help pick up all the kids who wanted to come see the Christmas play, and make it to the church in time before it started at 6:30pm.

Meanwhile, the rest of the family and I had a few more hours to spend, laughing at Uncle Rick's crazy jokes and antics.

My dad had arrived at the church about 6:10, with plenty of time to get all the kids in their seats before it started. At 6:25 my dad started calling my mom to ask where we were.

After a few missed calls, my mom finally answered the phone.

"Dear, where are you?" My dad said. "The Christmas play is about to start, and you still aren't here."

"What do you mean it's about to start? It begins at 7:00, right?" My mom replied.

"No, 6:30. Please hurry, or you're going to miss the play."

"Well, I thought the play started at 7:00, so we are about to head out the door," she replied.

There was something about that phone call that changed things. The mood altered significantly. Before the phone call, things were relaxed and calm. Everything was perfect. But after? Things felt different. The feeling of peace and comfort had been consumed by the pressure of being late and the anxiety that accompanied it.

THE WRECK

"Hey everyone, we have to hurry," My mom said. "The play is starting at 6:30, so we are already late!"

We were already dressed into our outfits that we were to wear for the play, so we hopped in the car, and headed to the church.

This was a day in my life that I will never forget.

My mom was driving. My brother and I were with her. All was well. My aunt was seated in the passenger seat, my uncle was seated directly behind the passenger seat, holding my cousin Rachel in his lap. My brother, Jonathan, was seated directly behind the driver's seat, and I was seated in the middle of the back seat between Uncle Rick and Jonathan.

Since we only lived approximately seventeen minutes from the church, we didn't see any issue with our seating arrangement. It was a packed car, sure, but it was for a short distance; my mom had always been known as an excellent driver.

The road through the valley in which we lived was constructed with gooseneck-like curves near the creek, and because our family had not lived in that area long, we were not aware that the road that we took to our house frequently had black ice on it. Even if my mom had been warned about the possibility of black ice, there was only one road for us to travel.

Finding Nathan

There was nothing she could have done differently to prevent what was to happen.

As I was seated in the middle of the backseat, I didn't really have a window to stare out of, so I kept my eyes focused through the front windshield and watched us drive down the curve-filled road.

Suddenly, my view changed.

No longer was I staring at the road in front of us, but I was now staring at the ditch we were headed directly for as we began to spin clockwise at approximately 40 mph.

The next and last thing I remember is the side of our car slamming directly into a utility pole and our car coming to a screeching halt – we went from 40 mph to 0 mph in a fraction of a second. A telephone pole came down. From the physical point of view, there was the screeching of breaks and the thunderous clash of metal. Our car had been transformed into a heap of mangled metal.

In a way, the car became a coffin.

That was the day my world turned upside down.

It was so fast.

It's impossible to believe how drastically life can change because of events that only take a few seconds.

THE WRECK

While I was knocked unconscious from the impact, my mom knew that everyone in the car was hurt. It was dark, one of the children in the back seat was gurgling and my Uncle Rick was calling her name. So she tried to get out of the car to get some help; yet, because of the way the car had crashed, her door was stuck shut. Determined to get help, she crawled over my aunt and was able to get out of the car through the passenger door. The road was blocked now and a man stopped and called 911. Another man, who happened to be an off-duty volunteer EMT, heard the call go out and rushed to the scene with some medical supplies and helped the rest of my family and me.

As I look back, it was a miracle that he was able to assist in helping us so quickly. While my mother wasn't as hurt as the rest of us, she was still in shock from the wreck and would not have had the strength to drag us out of the car and do all that the volunteer EMT did for us.

I am thankful that God had placed him there in that moment as it possibly saved our lives. My mom told me how all sorts of emergency response vehicles showed up including the fire department, police department, and multiple ambulances.

As the EMTs and paramedics rescued everyone from the car, one EMT asked her to help identify Jonathan and me. Because Jonathan and I were only eighteen months apart, we were very similar in size. Additionally, the impact of the accident had severely injured us both. The swelling and lacerations were so bad that Jonathan and I were practically indistinguishable from one another.

However, the EMTs did notice that Jonathan had on a hat. Thankfully, my mom knew whose hat it was and was able to identify Jonathan by his hat, which allowed the paramedics to administer age-appropriate treatment on us. I know that had to be a difficult time for my mother.

How could her two boys be injured so badly that they are completely unrecognizable and indistinguishable to her?

My uncle and aunt were shaken up, but fortunately, they did not have life-threatening injuries from the accident. My uncle was holding his young daughter in his lap when the accident happened, and miraculously, his daughter suffered no injuries except for a few scrapes and bruises. Uncle Rick did sustain a serious injury during the accident, but he was able to recover relatively quickly.

My mom, though shaken up, was able to walk away from the accident as well. This is in no way an attempt to minimize the injuries that my uncle, aunt, cousin Rachel, and my mom sustained, but the injuries to my brother and me were so severe and traumatic, that the injuries everyone else sustained seemed like a paper cut in comparison.

The Wreck

After the Christmas play was over, the pastor of our church explained to the congregation that my family had been in a car accident, and the church had a time of prayer. I am forever grateful for the support that my church showed to my family. The pastor assured my dad that the church would find someone else to help with the bus after the play and get everyone home who had ridden on the bus that night. A good family, who my parents were close friends with, offered to let my brother Daniel spend the night with them after the play was over, which was a blessing because my parents were not sure how long they were going to be at the hospital that night.

My dad, after making sure his responsibilities were going to be taken care of, headed to the hospital. He wanted to get to my family and me as quickly as possible. But, because he had parked his truck where he met our church bus, he was not able to immediately leave for the hospital. He had to get a ride from the church to the hospital – stunned, shocked, overwhelmed. The boys who had sat in his rocking chair were now seriously injured and on their way to two different hospitals.

My father talks about what he remembers:

> *I arrived at the hospital at approximately 8:35 PM. The ambulance arrived at the hospital carrying my brother, my sister-in-law, my niece, and my wife one minute before I arrived. I watched as the EMTs unloaded my brother; they were yelling at him to keep him awake. My wife climbed*

out of the front of an ambulance and came to my arms, sobbing. We walked into the hospital and waited on my brother and his wife who were getting CAT scans.

At approximately 10 PM I was approached and told I had a call from the Salem Hospital. Dr. Kim would like to speak to me. One of my sons had been sent to Salem Hospital. I said, "Hello this is Randy Jirovec." He said, "This is Dr. Kim, the neurosurgeon of Salem Hospital. I just finished operating on your son Jonathan – he is in stable condition. He has function on the left side of his body but not the right side. We have facilities only to do surgery; we do not have a trauma center for short-term or long-term care. He will need to be taken to OHSU. But let me advise you. There will be a risk. He can go by ground ambulance or by Life Flight." I asked, "What should I do." He said, "I cannot tell you what to do." "If it was your son, what would you do?" I asked. He said, "If it were my son I would Life Flight him to go." Immediately I said, "Life Fight to OHSU. Thank you, Dr. Kim."

I walked into a small bathroom in the hospital. Wearing my overcoat, I faced the mirror, put my hands on the edge of the sink, and bowed my head. I was in disbelief. All I said was, "Lord, help." After about a minute standing there, I felt a squeeze on my left shoulder. I looked up quickly in the mirror, but no one was there behind me. I looked at my left shoulder, and no one was there. I knew God was there for me and I knew I needed Him. I left the hospital at 11 PM and headed to OHSU where I would meet my two sons.

CHAPTER 4

The Hospital

Everyone in the car that had endured minor injuries was taken to the closest hospital, which was in McMinnville. Since McMinnville did not have the resources to handle the extensive traumas that my brother Jonathan and I had suffered. Jonathan was Life-Flighted to OHSU hospital in Portland; I was rushed by an ambulance to a hospital in Salem. After my mom was cleared from the hospital in McMinnville, someone drove my parents from McMinnville to OHSU in Portland and were able to learn more details about how the accident had actually occurred.

They both felt completely helpless.

There was no one to blame.

It wasn't anyone's fault.

Black ice is practically impossible to see, especially at night on a winding road. There was no one to blame. After the fact, hearing the details of the accident from my mom was almost unreal.

THE HOSPITAL

We all had to quickly come to grips with reality. My family had been in a terrible car accident. Even though we were all painfully aware that our worst nightmares were coming true, we felt as if we were in a dream.

I can only imagine how my parents must have felt knowing that we were severely injured but not having any idea as to how severe the injuries were. As my brother and I were both in surgery when they arrived at the hospital in Portland, they were unable to talk to any doctors about how we were. All they were able to do was sit and wait for someone to come out and tell us.

I hate to think about all that must have been running through my parents' heads as we were in surgery.

What if one of them doesn't make it?

What if they both don't make it?

If they do make it, what disabilities will they have to live with?

The feeling of helplessness had to have overwhelmed them. Imagine, your entire family was in a car wreck, and you have no idea if two of your sons are going to be okay or not, and there is nothing that you can do to change things. They must have felt as if there was nothing that they could do except sit and wait—- after all, they couldn't.

All the while, little did they know how bad the severity of the injuries Jonathan and I had actually sustained. I'm sure that they had hoped to find answers once they arrived at the hospital, but, no one, including the doctors, had any answers. Even though they had been able to process the flood of overwhelming information for nearly an hour, there was no way that they were ready to go through what they went through that night at the hospital. The only way that they must have made it through that night was by leaning on the grace of God.

When my parents arrived at OHSU at around 12:00am, they did not know what the long-term effects of the wreck we endured would be. By that time, Jonathan was on life support in the Intensive Care Unit (ICU). My parents spoke with the doctor who had been working with my brother Jonathan, and he told them that unfortunately, he was only being kept alive by the life support machine and that there had not been any brain activity since he had arrived at the hospital.

Still to this day I admire my father for having the bravery to make the right decisions at that moment. There I was, alive but brain-damaged. My father could either keep me alive but have me suffer massive long-term brain damage, or he could make the brave and bold decision to have me Life-Flighted to OHSU and run the risk of having me die in transit. I am thankful to both my father and Dr. Kim for being bold and making the right decision. It is because of God's grace and their decisions that I am able to write this book.

The Hospital

When I had arrived at OHSU, it was a huge relief for my parents to finally have their two sons in the same hospital. They no longer had the stress of having to talk to doctors and receive news over the phone. Although the surgery had been a success, the next several days were critical for me as the pressure on my brain had to be kept to a minimum to ensure that there was not any more brain swelling. My parents stayed up all hours with little to no sleep, constantly in prayer. I am thankful that I had parents that believed in prayer. Against all odds, God kept the pressure on my brain from rising. As the days passed, the pressure remained stable, and my parents remained thankful to God and in prayer every hour the pressure did not rise.

The morning I arrived at OHSU, the feelings of hope that my father had from my recovery were completely shattered. The doctors taking care of who they thought was me at the time but was actually Jonathan called my parents into Jonathan's room and told them that he was completely brain dead. His heart was failing. The only reason he was still breathing was because of the ventilator. They said there had been no sign of any brain activity since they put him on life support.

Did my parents want to leave him on life support and hope for a miracle or did they want to take him off of life support? Faced with this incredibly difficult decision, my parents asked the doctor if there was any chance that their son would recover. The doctor told them that, in his medical opinion, there was not.

I can only imagine how crushing this had to be for them. Not only did they have to suffer the loss of a child, but they ultimately had to make the choice to take him off of life support.

After taking an hour or so to think about and discuss what they wanted to do, my parents decided that they would allow the doctors to take him off of life support. The doctors allowed my parents to say their goodbyes before they turned off the machine.

My father whispered in his ear, "I love you." My mother whispered in his ear, "I love you. And I am so sorry." They were weeping.

Then they had to stand and watch Jonathan's body stop breathing.

The machine was off.

The noise dissipated.

The beeping stopped.

The heart monitor flat lined.

Their son's chest quit moving.

Their son, Jonathan, was dead.

My brother, Jonathan, was dead.

The Hospital

The hope that they must have had about my recovery must have seemed so far away as they stood in the hospital room and watched their son Jonathan pass away. Although we all believe that Jonathan had died at the scene of the accident, watching Jonathan's precious little body stop breathing is something that they say they will never forget.

My parents then left his room and walked down the hall. They entered my room, staring at me. I was on life support.

That night – which was supposed to be filled with joy and laughter as we celebrated Christmas with our church and family – turned out to be the most difficult night of our lives.

CHAPTER 5

My Funeral

If things weren't difficult enough for my parents, they soon would be.

My brother Jonathan had passed away, and they were forced with the burden of having to bury him.

Meanwhile, I was still mostly unconscious and in serious critical condition. Preparing for the funeral had to have been very difficult. It must have been a very emotional time for my parents. They had one son in the hospital with life threatening injuries, a nine-year-old son, Daniel, who they had to explain everything to, and a son whose funeral needed to be planned.

Fortunately, they had great support from friends and family that was very helpful throughout the process. But it was still an emotionally overwhelming and draining time. From picking the songs that would be sung at Jonathan's funeral to picking out his casket, they were having a very difficult week.

My Funeral

All the while they had no idea that the son they thought they were burying wasn't actually the son they were burying.

As mine and Jonathan's injuries were so severe, they were still under the impression that I was Jonathan and the son they were actually burying was me.

In other words, it wasn't Jonathan's funeral that they were having.

It was mine.

The day of my funeral with my name on it came: Thursday the 28th. It was only six days after our accident had occurred.

After the funeral, my parents still had many things that they had to deal with. As bad as my parents wanted to just sit at the graveyard and grieve over their lost son, they also wanted to be with me, as I was beginning to recover from the accident.

During the weeks after the accident, my mom lived at the hospital. My dad would go to work a few days and then come spend a couple days at the hospital with me. As much as he did not want to, he had to continue working.

Continuing to work is just one more reason that I admire him and all that he did for me. In the midst of one of the most difficult times anyone could even dream of going through, my dad still found the strength to go to work and financially support his family. Many people could not do what he did. But my dad is strong; he could do it.

The hospital had a Ronald McDonald house, which was an apartment complex for the family of children who were hospitalized long-term. That facility provided a small apartment with a private bedroom, bathroom, and a kitchen nearby. My mom being able to stay there was a huge blessing because we lived over an hour away from the hospital. One afternoon, Al McCandless's dad, Grandpa Mac, as we all called him, came by and shook my dad's hand and left $500 in his hand just to help out with expenses while our family was up at the hospital—what a huge blessing that was. A businessman, Paul Ables, pulled together businesses in the Portland area—they gave us approximately $7,000.

People just helped us fill in some gaps we had, and we could stay in Portland.

Meanwhile, my recovery had hit a standstill and had even gone into decline at certain points. Just when it seemed I was getting better, I would hit a low point. Eventually, I had gotten to the point where I was able to be moved out of ICU and into a normal hospital room, and I was able to fully wake up.

But I couldn't talk.

My Funeral

While I was in the hospital, my throat would swell up, which prevented me from breathing.

The nurses gave me a drug to relax my throat – I knew that was not working because, only a short time later, the same thing happened and I was once again unable to breathe.

My dad was able to pull a doctor into my room that was walking through the hallway, and after only looking at me for a minute, he noticed that I needed a tracheotomy. Within ten minutes, doctors came into my room and placed a tracheotomy in my throat, allowing me to breathe normally.

After this, I still could not talk.

This was a huge problem because not talking meant that I was unable to tell my parents that I was not Jonathan.

They kept calling me Jonathan.

I didn't exactly know why – I had to tell them!

But I couldn't.

The EMTs had put a tube down my throat that was too big for my throat, which scratched my vocal chords rendering me unable to speak. After a few weeks, I could barely muster a faint whisper.

The doctors told my parents that I would never be able to speak again. All hope seemed lost for me to be able to speak until one day we met with another doctor who thought he could help me regain my voice. The doctor told my parents that after I had healed up more, he thought he could do a procedure that could restore my voice. *Yes, Yes, Yes!* I thought. I couldn't express myself vocally, but hearing that I might one day be able to speak again filled me with joy. Joy that I had not felt since the accident.

I had not felt any sort of joy, only heartache and severe physical pain. But when I heard the doctor say there was a procedure that could be done to restore my voice, I finally had a feeling of joy. Thankfully, I could have the procedure, which removed scar tissue from my throat and allowed my voice to eventually come back. After I fully recovered, I was able to talk at about 90% of what I could before the accident. What a miracle!

I was in the hospital for a total of 57 days after the accident and, because I had a tracheotomy, I was unable to speak that entire time.

Finally, after a month and a half, I was able to come home for a day. My parents were so excited that I could come home even if it was only for one day. But the night I was home we had freezing weather, and we were unable to leave the house for a few days. The storm was actually a blessing because my return to the hospital was delayed, and I was able to stay longer than expected – although things were weird.

My Funeral

My parents were still calling me Jonathan.

I still didn't know why.

Did they think I was Jonathan?

What in the world was going on?

As a five-year-old, I had no idea what it meant. All I knew was that I had to tell them who I really was.

Although it was well past Christmas, I still had all my Christmas presents under the tree. Jonathan's presents were under there as well. Being a five-year-old, the first thing I did when I got home was to go to open up my presents. I ran over to the tree, found a gift-wrapped box that had my name on it and brought it to my parents to see if I could open it.

"Jonathan," they said. "Why did you grab Nathan's presents? Your presents are under the tree, too."

It was in that moment that I knew for sure that they thought that I was actually my brother. Although I was young, it was then that I also realized that who they thought they buried was actually me.

They told me that those presents were not mine and I could not have them, but that I could have my own presents.

Those are my own presents!, I thought.

FINDING NATHAN

The next day, Saturday, the Goforth family came to visit me (who they thought was Jonathan) at our house. The Goforth family was always very kind to Jonathan and had taken a liking to him, so they knew him very well. They had taken care of Jonathan six years before when my mother had surgery. As they were sitting talking with my mom, they told her that I was not Jonathan. My mom wasn't sure at first – she knew her sons better than friends did, but their remarks made her start thinking.

I was not fully recovered and had scars, but my mom assumed that I was actually Jonathan because she had already attended the funeral for her son Nathan.

Their suggestions started to bug her.

Saturday night, after the Goforth family left, we all sat down to dinner. Again, my mom had me sit where Jonathan usually sat but she could not get her conversation with the Goforth's out of her head.

It was cold in the room, so my dad got up to get a jacket. He also got a jacket for Jonathan.

My mom asked my dad who it was that was sitting next to him at the table.

He told her that that it was Jonathan, and he knew it because Jonathan had a scar on his nose from when he fell riding his bike when he was only a toddler. My dad was determined to get this confusion over with once and for all, so he walked over to me and began to look for the scar on my nose.

He looked, and he looked, but he could not see the scar.

His first reaction was that some surgery he had had after the car accident had somehow made the scar disappear. He thought a miracle occurred—the scar had vanished.

Then, it hit him. He put his hands on both sides of my face and asked the question I had been waiting to hear:

"Who are you? Are you Jonathan?"

I vigorously shook my head back and forth, left to right, indicating NO!

He was shocked as he replied, "You are Nathan?"

I shook my head up and down, which meant YES!

Flabbergasted, he repeated my question, "You are Nathan?"

Again, I shook my head up and down—YES!

That moment was when it truly sank in – the boy they had thought was dead, and they had buried weeks prior was actually sitting right in front of them. It was me, Nathan.

My entire family immediately began crying – weeping for joy! I was alive!

My parents could not believe it. In their minds, it was like their boy had been raised from the dead. They all rejoiced that night, and the elation could not have been higher.

But wait, if Nathan was alive, then Jonathan had gone to heaven. The raw emotion of loss hit them all over again.

My dad woke with a shock the next morning at 3:00am. The reality of it fully sunk in.

Jonathan was gone.

We had buried Jonathan.

The grieving hit hard … again.

A week later we held a memorial service for Jonathan. The Goforth family sang.

***

As I have reflected back to the weeks after the accident occurred, I almost cannot believe that my parents did not catch onto the fact that I was Nathan much earlier than they did. It took a friend questioning my identity to make them consider which son they had buried and which son was alive.

My Funeral

Even though I was alive, I was not out of the woods just yet; I had a long road to recovery ahead of me.

Despite my condition, I was still an independent, fun little boy. While we were home, I would roll around in my wheelchair on our deck, and I would roll down an eight-inch step onto the concrete. I must admit, my plan did not work well, and my wheelchair flipped forward. My dad had to pick up the wheelchair, and he told me that I could not try and go down steps in my wheelchair without help.

But I decided that after the wreck, I was not going to live a life in a state of self-pity because of my permanent injuries. Even in a wheelchair, I was going to always push myself to the limits. I returned to the hospital for about a week before I was finally discharged for good, and my parents made the decision that they were going to treat me just like they treated our other son, Daniel.

They did not want to raise me thinking that I should get special treatment because I had some permanent injuries. Their decision to help but not coddle me, coupled with the determination that I had to build myself a successful, normal life, resulted in me growing up and becoming an educated entrepreneur who always finds a way to accomplish whatever lofty goals that I have set for myself.

I am thankful for the decision my parents made to treat me as if I had no disabilities whatsoever.

It taught me to never make excuses and that giving up is never an option.

Left to Right, Back row: Dawn, Rick, Rachel, Jonathan, Randy, Shirley

Front row: Daniel and Nathan

Left to Right: Dawn, Rick, Rachel, Daniel, Nathan, Randy, Shirley

CHAPTER 6

My Mother

My mother has suffered more than any of us. Her endurance through all that she has gone through is remarkable. In fact, it wasn't until years after the accident that she was able to discuss what happened to us as a family. Throughout the healing process, she felt as if it was somehow her fault. She has felt as if she could have avoided the wreck from ever happening. As much as we tell her the blame is not on her, she has a hard time accepting what has happened to our family.

She was the one in the driver's seat.

She was the one that wasn't severely injured when others were.

However, there wasn't anything she could have done to prevent the wreck. The black ice on the road was completely unforeseeable, and it is entirely unrealistic to expect her to have seen it.

I often put myself in her shoes. I try and imagine how she has felt throughout this process of recovery.

FINDING NATHAN

Just imagine, you are driving your family to church – they all count on you to get them there safely. Then your car begins to slip on the frozen road beneath you, and you completely lose control of the wheel and the direction of the vehicle. You try helplessly to slam on the brakes, but the brakes don't work. The car slides and turns sideways at 45 miles per hour and wraps itself around a utility pole. You're okay, and you realize what just happened. Fearing the results of your actions, you have no idea what to expect when you look to your right or when you look behind you. Things will no longer be the same – that much you do know.

You look to your right, and your family member in the passenger seat is lying there conscious but hurt. Everything is dark. It is difficult to make out the condition of those in the backseat. You don't know if they are dead or severely injured. You hear your brother-in-law calling your name. You hear your niece crying. Your two sons are lying there severely injured – you can't even seem to make out which one is which. You hear one of the boys gurgling.

I cannot even imagine the fear that my mother must have felt to see my brother Jonathan and me lying there unconscious.

When she looked in the back seat, she also had seen my uncle holding my little cousin in his lap. The fact that my little cousin was not injured is beyond miraculous. Weighing less than 50 pounds, she could have easily been thrown out the window and killed.

But instead, God saved her life. I thank God every day that it was me that was injured and not her, or that it was me that was injured and not my uncle or my mom. I certainly think they are all strong enough to deal with what I have gone through, but I would never want them to.

My road has not been easy.

It has not been short.

It has been long and filled with tragedy and unpredictability.

I'm happy and delighted to be here today to tell you that my life is a blessing, that through all that I have been through, through all that has happened, God has found a way to bring me out the other side. God has found a way to help me achieve all of my dreams and goals.

Everything that I wanted to achieve before my wreck, I can still reach. It is not by my own effort that I can do these things, but by God's amazing grace. By His strength alone, I can do far more than I was told I would be capable of doing, and by God's strength alone, my mom continues to be a wonderful mother despite all that she has been through.

My mother, while she was not injured in the wreck, probably has suffered even more than I have. She has suffered so much loss and heartbreak. She has dealt with a burden that no parent should ever have to go through, yet she does everything for us. She's the toughest lady I know and to have her as my mom is a blessing. In 2000 God gave my mom and dad a new son and me a new brother. His name is David. David was Jonathan's middle name.

I often ask myself why this wreck happened. Why I have to suffer and endure all that I have to. I ask why God chose for my family to go through this. I simply ask why.

Slowly, God is giving me the answer, and one thing is for sure:

But by the grace of God I am what I am: and his grace which was bestowed upon me was not in vain; but I labored more abundantly than they all: yet not I, but the grace of God which was with me (Corinthians 15:10, KJV).

This is such a beautiful verse. I am what I am today because of the grace of God. He is the supplier of my strength, and He is the supplier of my mom's strength.

With all that she has been through, for her to still keep her faith is remarkable. So many times we hear stories of other parents that have gone through the loss of a child and have started to spiritually and emotionally fall apart. My mother did not do that, but it's easy to see how one would.

My Mother

For a lot of parents who have children, those children become their life. And when the child dies, and the parent has to bury their child, the parent feels as if they died with them. I thank God that my mom was able to hold on to her strength and to help me to grow as a person.

My mom worked extremely hard to give me a better life and to not let my disabilities hold me back. My mom has worked so hard to hold on to her relationship with my brother, Daniel, and my dad as well. She is indeed an example of what it means to be a caring mother and a caring wife.

So many times, parents who lose a loved one fall apart. They lose the emotional connection that they once had with their spouse, the intimate relationship they once had. In the case of many couples, any time they get close with one another, they are reminded with the death of their son.

But fortunately, not only did my parents refuse to grow apart from one another, but they actually grew closer. They are now closer than they've ever been. They have found a way, through God, to not let tragedy in their lives tear them apart.

Through tragedy, they have strived to become a better husband and a better wife, and they have succeeded. Through tragedy, they have strived to become a better mother and father, and they have succeeded.

Instead of being reminded of Jonathan's death anytime they get closer to one another, they are reminded of Jonathan's life, his wonderful personality, his exuberant nature, and his unique ability to make people smile. For my parents to have grown closer is just wonderful, and it has been essential for me to grow as an individual and as a person.

I don't know where I would be, or how I would be, if they weren't such a strong influence in my life. If they had not been resilient throughout the process, if they didn't show me the example of how to live through tragedy, I would not have been able to overcome and accomplish the things that I have been able to overcome and accomplish.

Again, my mom is one of the strongest women I know. She also lost a child – David's twin – during pregnancy. Through all of these difficulties, she has not only kept her faith but has grown in her faith and put God first through it all. She is always singing or humming hymns that remind her of hope. She has set an example for everyone in my family. She has shown us how to keep God first in life, to trust in Him through difficult times, and to hope that the result will be God's will.

CHAPTER 7

Jonathan's Story

My mom is one of the strongest ladies I know and my dad is one of the strongest men I know. Through them, I have an instilled strength to overcome all that I have had to go through. Through them, they instilled the strength to my brother, Daniel, to go through all that he has gone through.

Why my brother Jonathan had to die, I don't know and probably never will. But I do know that even through his story, people will find comfort. I know that I am here today to not only tell my story but to also tell my mom and dad's story. Even more than my mom and my dad's story, I am here to tell my brother Jonathan's story – to tell the story of the one that doesn't have a voice. Through his death, I want people to understand that they have life and to appreciate the life that they have.

Jonathan was the most kind-hearted person I know, and I know if it the roles were switched, as they once were, then he would handle the situation perfectly. He would deal with his sorrow and grief by seeking love from those around him. He would deal with his sorrow and grief by taking action on the things that he cares most about, and more than anything else, he would deal with his sorrow and grief by seeking God first, above all else.

I try to live a life that he would live, as I know if I can be half the person that he would have turned out to be then I will have lived a life well lived.

It is crucial that we all be who God created us to be. I also believe that having role models and good examples of character in your life are important for you to develop into the best person you can be. I believe that we should all seek to find someone in our lives that we can learn from and use as an example to go about our lives on a daily basis, whether that is a brother, parent, or a role model in our lives. Regardless of who we learn from, we all have one person that we can share as a prime example of how to live a meaningful life: Jesus Christ.

I believe that this example isn't just limited to Christians alone, but if we all were to take an in-depth look at the gospels, as I have done many times throughout my journey, I think that we can find that Jesus Christ is a flawless example of a life worth living. We often have a tendency to put ourselves above all else and to put ourselves above everyone else – its human nature.

However, Jesus never put Himself first in anything He did. While Christ was on earth, He put God first and

His neighbor second; never once did He consider what was best for Him. If Jesus had denied being the Messiah, He would have avoided the punishment He received, or if Jesus had called on God to send angels to His rescue while on the cross, He would have avoided the punishment He received.

Instead, Jesus endured the suffering, for our sake, because He loves us so very much. He loves me; He loves you; He loves all of us. Jesus never did anything to deserve the punishment He received, but instead, He suffered the punishment we deserved so that we would never have to.

As many times as I hear the gospel, this part always speaks to me so very loudly. Jesus suffered an unjust punishment so that we wouldn't have to pay for what we inevitably deserved.

He took the fall for us. For that, I believe that I owe Him my life, and I believe that I owe Him every part of my life. I'm writing to you because I want you to realize that Jesus didn't just die for me, or for the rich, or the poor, or the disabled, or the extremely intelligent, or the illiterate, but instead, He died for all of us. All of us have fallen short of His perfect standard, and because of that, we are all sinners unworthy of His forgiveness, but God looks passed it all. In God's eyes, we are His children, and we are perfect in the eyes of God.

All we have to do is cry out to Him, and He will handle the rest.

FINDING NATHAN

It is easy for us to praise God when things are easy, when all is going well.

What about when disaster strikes?

The natural inclination for me, as well as for a lot of people, is to question God during tragedy. It is to get mad at God. The natural inclination is to say: "I put my trust in Him, and He let me down."

There are many times throughout my journey – through the wreck, through the recovery, through the rehabilitation, and through my overall growth to where I am today – that I have gotten angry with my current circumstances. So many times, I have longed to just be normal. I have wanted things to come easier for me. So many times, I have had to do small tasks that take me forever, and I have just wanted to be able to do them in a normal amount of time, like normal people.

In these moments of weakness, the low moments, there are two options: pray or run. I choose to pray, and every time I do – while sometimes it isn't immediate – I find peace and understanding. Romans 8:28 says: "And we know that all things work together for good to them that love God, to them who are the called according to his purpose" (Romans 8:28, KJV). It doesn't say *all good things,* but it says *all things* – good and bad.

God can use every trial in our lives as a testament.

Jonathan's Story

The tragedy and heartbreak that I have been through, as well as that of my family, have led me here to writing this book. The disaster in my life has given me a story; it's given me purpose. I now have the calling to reach out to those who are in a similar circumstance, who are going through tragedy as well.

There was a story I heard one time of a little girl that had accidentally been shot in a crossfire by a criminal. She was rushed to the hospital, and they did not believe that she would survive the wound. They rushed the little girl into surgery and found that the bullet was a quarter of an inch from her heart, but she was fine. The surgeon also found a tumor that could have been potentially life-threatening to her down the road. A tumor that would never have been spotted if she had not been shot. The surgeon removed the tumor, and the girl was fine.

In the moment after the gunshot, there was seemingly no good thing that could come from it. When we don't know what the answer to crisis is, we can take solace in the knowledge that God cares for us and is working everything for our benefit. God can repair any situation and work every situation for the good of those who love Him.

There was an analogy I heard one time of a man that was in good relationship with God, and he followed God and walked with God. It paints a picture of this man actually walking with God and there are two separate sets of footprints – the man's footprints and God's footprints. But the guy noticed that whenever tragedy occurred in his life, there was only set of one footprints, so the guy asked God: "Why is it that when tragedy occurs in my life, I am the only one walking? Why do you leave me when bad things occur? God, you are only with me through the good times!" To this, God replied: "My son, when tragedy occurs, it is then that I carry you."

Even when it seems like God has abandoned us, it is usually in those moments that God has never held us closer.

CHAPTER 8

My Purpose, My Pastor, and Daniel

Why did this happen?

Why did this wreck take place?

Where do we go from here?

These are questions that I am not sure I will ever be able to answer, but I know that God has a purpose. He not only has a purpose for me and everyone else involved with the wreck, but it is for everyone in this world – including you.

Everyone has a story.

Everyone has to overcome adversity in their lives.

Everyone struggles with something.

It's easy to say that my struggles are much greater – perhaps they are, but my purpose is not necessarily greater. We all have a responsibility to tell our story of what has happened in our lives and how God has used those either positive or negative events in our lives. We have a responsibility to share God's word about what we have been through. We have all experienced loss in our lives and have been through a difficult time. But through it all, we find something much greater than ourselves. We have seen how much stronger we are than we think. We have seen how strong God is. We have seen how strong God can make a weak man.

I don't know why the wreck happened, and I don't think I ever will. But I trust that God will continue to bring me peace and understanding.

Part of His plan is for me to encourage you to tell your story.

Whatever it may be, tell your story. If you're at a place right now where you don't feel like you have a story to tell, if you are at a place like I was when I was lying in the hospital room unable to speak and having recently lost my brother, I would say to keep believing.

There is a light at the end of the tunnel, and I can promise you that God has a plan for your life. One of the main reasons for the development of depression in people is the feeling of not having a purpose. So many people nowadays feel as if they have no reason to live; this is due to a lack of purpose. I sincerely believe that we all have purpose to the same extent as everyone else around us, but I also believe that the purpose is found in God and nothing else. When we seek purpose that is separate from God, we seek purpose that was never intended for us to go after.

There are numerous stories of people who have chased their dreams, achieved their dreams, and ultimately felt purposeless. I believe that this is because when we chase dreams that God never intended for us to chase, we are chasing dreams that will give us temporary satisfaction and will ultimately leave us feeling unsatisfied. But when we chase desires that God has placed upon our hearts, we are chasing a purpose that will ultimately yield eternal satisfaction – and that, my friend, is why purpose can only truly be found in Christ.

Why do people abuse drugs? They understand that they will ultimately suffer greatly, perhaps by way of death, if they do so. They abuse drugs because of the temporary pleasure they get from doing so. They abuse drugs because of the euphoric feeling of peace and pleasure they get from it. However, they fail to realize that they can have everything they search for through drugs, all the good they feel while high, in a relationship with God.

Except, with God, they have it times a thousand and for all of eternity.

The pastor that was pastoring me on that tragic day 22 years ago still helps me and the rest of my family through the difficult process today. His time spent as pastor at the same church speaks very highly to the dedication he has in fulfilling God's word and God's plan for his life. He has been deeply committed to the word of God and doing God's will. He knows, like I know, that God has a plan for everything that happens in life and that God has a purpose for everyone who was involved in this wreck. He also truly understands what his purpose is.

His purpose has been not to only help us, to help me, my mom, my dad, and my brother Daniel, but to also help everyone who has been his congregation that was struggling with something. They may not have been struggling with the death of a family member, but with something. Everyone in our church has struggled with something, and he was there for them when they need to talk about it. He knew that he needed to be there for them, and he was there for them every day.

Anyone in our church could call him, and he would answer. There has never been a time when someone in our family called him and he did not answer. There has never been a time when someone had been through a difficult time and he had not been there for them, completely - where he has not given himself for the cause of recovery. He has truly been a blessing to our family. He is an example for every pastor on how to care for his congregation. He is especially an example for me. He has shown me how to go about living a meaningful life filled with purpose and how to fulfill the purpose that God has for my life.

Pastors are held to such a high standard, but like everyone, they sometimes mess up. For my pastor to live up to all the expectations that have been placed upon him is truly remarkable. For my pastor to always be there for his congregation, regardless of what is going in his own life or what type of day he is having, is truly inspirational.

I think so many times we forget that pastors need encouragement and recognition for their good work. I feel as if, nowadays, many pastors aren't fully appreciated for all that they do.

Whereas many Christians will only sacrifice a Sunday morning as long as the service doesn't go too long, pastors have sacrificed their entire lives for the gospel, for the sake of heaven. I think it's important that we recognize all that our pastors do for us and the level of service that they provide to so many people, and above all else, we, too, need to remember that they need to be prayed for more than anyone. We always think about how it is the pastor's responsibility to pray for his congregation, but it is also the congregation's responsibility to pray for the pastor, as they need Godly strength more than anyone. I want to recognize pastors across this country that commit fully to their work for God as they are so important to the ones that they impact.

Also, my brother Daniel has been through a very difficult time, just as difficult as any of us. He had to sit at someone else's house in our church and know that both of his brothers might die, but not know if they would, when they would, or how they would. Then he had to live with the pain of my injuries and long painful recovery and of Jonathan's death.

Like my mother, the wreck has taken a very emotional toll on him.

If he had been there, would Jonathan not have died?

Would he have taken his place?

This idea is one that still bothers Daniel to this day. To sit second hand and watch everything unfold the way that it has unfolded has been very tough for my brother. He also, like my mother, has a difficult time speaking about the accident, but his faith slowly grows. We pray for him daily.

All the while, my brother has always been there for me and has always put my and my parents needs above his. He is one of the most selfless people I know, and I pray that he learns to open up throughout the ongoing process because, even twenty years later, it still bothers him, which I believe points to his wonderful spirit. It points to his compassionate nature and to his loving heart. The fact that he cares so much it hurts over twenty years after what we went through as a family is a testament to who he is.

It bothers him that I had to go through the heartbreak, physical trauma, and emotional trauma that I've had to go through. It bothers him that I had to go through all that, and he never even had a scratch. He would give his life for me; I know he would. He would trade places for me if he could. He deeply cares. If he could go back, he would take my place. I know that without a doubt in my mind. Like I said, I couldn't ask for better parents, and I couldn't ask for a better brother.

Daniel has been an excellent brother, and he has not treated me any differently because of my disabilities. He has treated me as if I have never had a scratch. Because of this, I thank him. It is through treating me as if I don't have any disabilities that I have learned to do things at a normal rate. It is through treating me normal that I can accomplish all that normal people can. Although it may take a little longer, I can still do them.

Without him constantly pushing me to be better than I am, I am not sure I would have ever accomplished anything that I have been able to accomplish in my life.

CHAPTER 9

A Relationship with God

The journey that I would go through immediately following the recovery process was very difficult and a major challenge to my faith.

Sometimes, people that have been through something like what I have been through and have kept their faith make it look so easy. They make it look like trusting God is the easy thing to do during tragedy. It is inspiring to see people who think or feel that trusting God is the easy way.

But, for me, it wasn't that easy.

There were times that I questioned God throughout the healing process. There were times when I felt like I didn't have anything to live for. Sometimes, it felt like the injuries that I endured, the disabilities that I would now have to live with, were too great, and God could not fix my problems. Sometimes, I was mad at God, and I would cry out and ask him why I went through all that I had gone through. So, although God was right there with me the entire time, I can't say that my faith was easy to come by.

I can say that my family was in the same place, too.

My dad always looked like he knew everything was in God's hands, and he truly believed that, I know. But there is a difference in believing without a doubt and believing with a doubt. I think we, as a family, choose to believe because we believe that God is in control – even when it is sometimes hard.

I guess that is why they call it faith.

They call it faith because it's what you can't see, it's what you don't know. You just have to believe while not ever knowing for sure – that's faith. That's what I know I have struggled with, and that's what the rest of my family has struggled with as well. My dad struggled, even though he looked like he didn't. He didn't want us to see his weak moments, but his son was just taken away from him. He didn't know if his other son was going to live or not, and he didn't know if that other son was going to be able to walk or talk again if he did live. If I could walk and talk, my dad didn't know if I would ever be able to have a normal childhood, be able to do things on my own, or be able to have any sort of independence. It's so easy in those moments to question God, and I don't think that it's unhealthy to question God in those moments. It's important to realize that God is there even through all of our pain. Even through all our uncertainty, God understands. He is not mad at us for feeling anger. It is natural. Part of our human nature is to be angry at bad things that happen that we don't understand. God doesn't call us to never be angry. God calls us to worship him and to trust in him no matter how hard it may be and to keep our faith in Him through all of our struggles despite our anger.

I thank God that I had parents that were able to keep their faith through their pain. I think of my mom. She still has hurt inside of her that she is slowly letting go of. That does not make her a bad person. She understands that God has a purpose through the wreck, and God has a purpose for her and my life. While she doesn't understand things, and while not understanding can bother her and lead to a feeling of anger, a feeling of bitterness and just sadness, she understands that God is still in control. She understands that God still has a plan for her life. She finds joy knowing that Jonathan is waiting for her in heaven and that her story is a testament to God.

I think the story of Job. God took Job, who had so much, and took everything from him. He took everything – well almost everything. There is one thing of Job's that God did not take – his family. God did not touch Job's family. He did not break up Job's relationship with his family, but instead, God left his family and friends. Although his friends and family felt anger, resentment, and bitterness at what Job had to suffer through, Job kept his faith and honored God.

A Relationship with God

While, at times, Job's family thought about abandoning God, God never condemned or cursed them for speaking poorly of him. It was all a test of family, and, in my own life, all of our struggles that we have been through as a family – that I have been through personally – is very similar to the story of Job.

As I study the bible, I see that God never changes.

My purpose, your purpose, everyone's purpose is just as meaningful in the eyes of God. We all have a purpose, and we should all seek to fulfill that purpose.

What does it mean to live a happy life?

This is a question that so many people struggle with and a question that I believe almost everyone nowadays is faced with.

Why am I not happy?

What does it take to be happy?

Although it is hard to say what the answer to these questions is, I know what the answer isn't. So many people chase material things, thinking that it will lead to happiness. So many times, I hear, "Oh. if I only had this I would be happy," and they are always chasing more and more and more, and what seems to happen is they will acquire more, and it still won't be enough. So they will get more, and it won't be enough. So they will get more, and it still won't be enough.

In my life, it isn't about chasing more and accomplishing all that I can for my own benefit.

Going through what I have been through, and enduring and suffering through all that I have endured and suffered through, has made me grateful to have life. It has shown me that there is something beautiful about just being alive, about just being able to thank God for another day here on earth.

I think that true joy is found in contentment.

So many people are not content with who they are or where they currently are in life.

So many people are looking for more, for better.

They are looking for the answers in all of the wrong places. They say. "If I can just be married, then I'll be happy." Or "If I can just have a child, then I'll be happy." And then they have a child and their goal is now to have another child in order to find happiness.

Discontentment can be found in all areas of life. Take one's career for example. I hear: "If I can just get this job, then I'll be happy." Then they will get the job, and it becomes "If I just get the promotion then I'll be happy." Then they get the promotion, and they want another promotion and another promotion. We are constantly seeking approval and are constantly seeking things that will never fully satisfy us.

A Relationship with God

Having been through all that I have been through, I realize now that happiness is found when you just let go. There is something so powerful about letting go. There is something so wonderful and so spiritually awakening about simply letting go of everything and dropping all that you have. I think whenever we come to the point where we just let go, where we quit chasing material items, where we quit chasing things that we will never find, and when we quit chasing more and more and more of this life, we will be happy. When we put God first and know that God will provide us with all that we need, it is then that we will find happiness in this life. That's when we find inner peace and the spiritual serenity that can only be found in God.

God works in mysterious ways. That's a saying that a lot of people reference and a lot of people talk about, and it has certainly been true in my own life. The earthly thing to think is that happiness is found in more, but there is something so beautiful about finding happiness in losing everything. On the surface, on the outside looking in, it could be said that my life should not be a happy life. That all I have been through should hold me back from living my life with fulfillment.

Fulfillment – a word that is so often misused.

Fulfillment is not filling your life with all these material items, but living a life fulfilled is living a life filled with God.

FINDING NATHAN

God has taken away so much in my life, and it is so true that in losing it all, in losing so much, so much is found.

While it hurts that I've lost so much, I still believe that, through it all, I have found so much.

I have realized how much I have through the loss of so much.

It is through losing so much that I realize how much I have.

CHAPTER 10

Stepping into the Unknown

We all experience the loss of loved ones at some point in our lives; my testimony is nothing new.

Sadly, I think so many people deal with it in the wrong way.

Many turn to the bottle to drown their sorrows; many choose to suppress their burdens without ever talking about their feelings. So many fail to do two things: turn to God and discuss their feelings. Many think that they are okay and that they do not need to discuss the situation, yet, it's obvious they are going through something.

From what I've seen from those who hide their sorrows in the bottle or try to bury them deep down inside is that they become very bitter. They might turn from a person that is very caring for others and live life with enthusiasm and excitement to a person who is critical of others and goes through life with little ambition. The effects, while obvious to the ones around them, are usually hard to identify by the ones who are struggling with grief.

I think it is crucial that when going through grief, you should try and open up about your feelings and discuss what you are going through. When you do so, you start to feel better. You start to feel as if a weight has been lifted off of your shoulders. Your attitude and spirit seem renewed, and you can begin to realize the purpose that God has for your life.

I am certainly not the perfect example of what I am writing – I have a very difficult time opening up about my story – but I'm doing my best to tell my story.

I'm doing my best to tell my story, not only for my benefit but also because I know that if I tell my story to enough people for a long enough time, then I will reach somebody.

If I reach just one person through my story, if I can somehow encourage at least one person to seek God through the midst of their struggles, then my purpose has been fulfilled – which is what it's all about.

Our time here on earth will prove to be such a short amount of time when we are in heaven. The thing that matters most is how we lived and who we impacted given the opportunity. If we can impact just one life, if we can help one person to Jesus, then we have done so much more than we could ever believe. As it says in Luke 15:10, "Likewise, I say unto you, there is joy in the presence of the angels of God over one sinner that repenteth" (Luke 15:10, KJV).

So for that, the way we live, the words we use, and the facial expressions we carry can have an eternal consequence. Choose to be a good example because you never know who is watching you, and if we can help one sinner repent, even then do angels in heaven rejoice.

The moments right before I would start my rehabilitation and recovery were terrifying. I had no clue what to expect or what I would now be like. The only thing that I knew for certain was that nothing would be the same. I wouldn't walk the same, talk the same, or even look the same.

"Normal" is a word that would no longer be applied to my life.

I remember being so scared of what my future would hold that it would keep me up at night. I remember being so frightened of what my parents would now have to go through and what they have already been through, that I would lie awake for endless hours of the night doing nothing but praying for them, my brother, and myself.

One thing that I learned from that experience is that fear is extremely emotionally powerful; it's even crippling at times. I also learned one other thing through those restless nights: fear has no real power; it's all in your head.

Fear can punch you harder than just about anything else if you let it, but you don't have to let it. Fear cannot touch you physically and can be overcome by taking action, by attacking the very thing that you are afraid of. I was afraid of what I could not accomplish when I was newly disabled – making good grades, being able to provide for myself financially and independently, and being the same warm, loving family member that I had always been before.

Instead of running from these things as many times fear leads us to do, I decided to attack and take action. I decided to do everything in my power to be a good student, and while it took me much longer than I wanted to get the results I wanted, I was able to make good grades. I decided to make sure I could provide for myself financially, even though my parents never required me to, so I started a business – a successful business, I might add, and one that I am really proud of.

And above all else, I put my God and my family above anything I did for myself.

The main lesson that I took away from my struggles is that while fear can be damaging and destructive to one's psyche, it can also be the very thing that drives one to do things that they never fathomed being able to do.

I never thought that I would be able to accomplish all that I have, but I went after my dreams.

Stepping into the Unknown

God has led me to places that only He saw as possible.

I hear so many stories of people who overcome fear, and they are all miraculous. I hear of people who have a severe fear of heights, so they climb mountains. I know some people who were extremely shy and too anxious to speak in front of crowds but who are now leading congregations as pastors. They attacked their fears and became wonderful public speakers. I know doctors that started out as subpar students but attacked their fears by doing all that they can to make good grades.

Whatever the fear may be, it can be overcome by ambition and determination. So many times we think that our weaknesses define who we are, and we accept them. But I say that our weaknesses can become strengths. As the verse in 2 Corinthians states: "And he said unto me, My grace is sufficient for thee: for my strength is made perfect in weakness. Most gladly therefore will I rather glory in my infirmities, that the power of Christ may rest upon me" (2 Corinthians 12:9, KJV). God makes strengths out of our weaknesses; it's one reason why our God is so magnificent. We have weaknesses – not to serve as roadblocks that aren't to be crossed, but, instead, as barriers that are meant to be overcome.

Whatever your weaknesses are, you can overcome them.

Conclusion: Life Now

I thank God for the opportunity He gave me to go on a mission trip. Without His grace, I never could have done it. But I can honestly say it changed my life. First I went to the Philippians and stayed there about a week.

A pastor friend from Arkansas was there, and he arranged for me to go and meet a missionary family in Baguio City. I was going to meet the pastor and his wife, but they were gone on one of their mission trips. The pastor's family showed me around the city and took me to some missionary churches that they are involved in. God is doing a mighty work through this family's ministry. They have started eleven churches there and are currently involved in all of them.

After that, I went back down to Manila, where the pastor from Arkansas was staying. He was a guest speaker at a conference. I stayed there for two days and heard some good preaching. In total, I spent about a week in the Philippines and then went to India.

In India, we went with a pastor to his children's home, which had about forty children –twenty boys and twenty girls. He showed us around the home. It had two floors. The first floor was where the children slept. The rooms they have are not big, but they make do with what they have. Upstairs there is a big room where all the children sit as they eat their plate of rice and curry chicken. A bowl is put in the middle of the room and they pass their plates in to get some food. They use a big spoon to get the rice and curry chicken with, but other than that, they use their hands to eat. We all ate and had a short service there. Before the service, all the children sang for us, and it was beautiful. We stayed a little longer there because we had a nurse that wanted to check all the children out.

While we were waiting for the nurse to get done, a little girl was looking at me and smiling. To keep her attention, I started moving my Adam's apple up and down, and she started giggling. She then nudged her friend and pointed at me, and her friend started laughing at me as well. Before long, everyone was laughing and looking at me. They were having a good time. I even got the nurse to look at me and say,

"What are you doing to make them laugh?" I told her what I was doing and she rolled her eyes at me. She then went back to what she was doing. After she had finished, we left. It was hard for me to leave, I hope I get to go back and see them soon.

We got to see several people give their lives to the Lord after we preached to them at one church we visited. Though they don't have much, they do have Jesus Christ in their hearts. Some churches there are like carports with blankets wrapped around them, yet in the U.S. we think it's bad if we have a little speck on the floor. Many of their churches have dirt floors.

My greatest struggle wasn't physical; it was leaving the children.

My heart goes out to those children.

They may not have much, but you never see them with a frown on their faces.

They are all precious to me – each one of them.

I hope that in the near future, I get to go back and see them. God is doing a great work there. I love each and every one of them.

As I look back, I wonder. Would I care for these people if I had not had the wreck?

What would my life be like without the wreck?

Would it be better?

That's the question that weighs heavily on my mind. That's the question that is hard for me to grasp.

I think so much about my brother Jonathan and how life would be if that wreck wouldn't have happened.

If that black ice had not been on the road, Jonathan would be here with us today. It's hard to imagine that he is gone. As happy as I am in life, I still think about what it would be like if the wreck had never happened; if I never suffered the disabilities that I suffered. More importantly, I think about life if Jonathan had never died. I often wonder what that would be like. I imagine a normal life having my brothers and never being challenged to go the extra mile just to do something that is routine for someone else. I would never have realized how wonderful my parents are.

Would I have become complacent?

Would I have taken what I have for granted?

I don't know. But there is one thing I do know: my story would never have been told. It's not that I wouldn't have a story to tell or that I wouldn't have purpose. I would, and we all do, but I wouldn't have realized how important it is to tell that story. What I want to encourage you to understand is not to wait for tragedy to strike you to move for God.

Don't wait for something supernatural, something bigger than we are to move us. God created us to work for Him and to spread His word.

God created us to tell our story, and whatever that is, we need to tell it. It would be awesome and wonderful to have Jonathan here, and just imagining him here brings tears to my eyes. I miss him so much.

But I have a responsibility to tell his story.

I have a responsibility to tell my story, and that's what I'm going to do. I hate that he isn't with us, but I wouldn't go as far as to say that my life would be more fulfilled if he was here. That isn't to say that his death was a good thing because it certainly was not, but it is just miraculous to see how something so bad can be used by God to do so much good and reach so many lives.

I feel His purpose is for me to tell my story.

I feel His purpose is for me to tell Jonathan's story, and that's why I'm here.

That's why I'm writing to you.

Even when people stare. Even when people wonder what happened. I am still *Finding Nathan.*

I am speaking for the ones who don't have a voice.

I am encouraging you to tell your story no matter how small or how big you think it is.

No matter how significant or insignificant you think it is, find your Nathan and tell your story. I want you to understand that it is important that you tell your story because it will reach somebody.

It is important that you pray about your purpose and that you try to get an understanding of what God wants you to do with your life.

A Personal Note from Nathan

What is life, in the Bible it tells us, "it is even a vapor, that appeareth for a little time, and then vanisheth away". James 4:14.

In life we have family, friends and neighbors to fill in the gaps in our hearts, but there is something else missing in our hearts. A longing to know more, spiritually, we have what we need physically but spiritually we are missing. That longing is what created and made you for His pleasure. His name is Jesus Christ and He was so in love with you as He created you that He came down and lived a sinless life and was an example to all those around Him. He healed many, many people and told them that He was the Creator of the world, which He is and that He loves each of them.

Then He was convicted and tried and was sentenced to death for not doing anything wrong at all. But after He died on the cross and they put Him in a tomb, He arose the third day and now He is seated by His Father(God the Father), and He wants to take your place on that cross if you will let Him, which He took my place on that rugged cross. He does not want you when you die to go to a place that He made for Satan and his angles, because He is Perfect and Holy and sin is wicked and wrong in His sight and He cannot look at it, but He is Holy and True.

A Personal Note from Nathan

He wants you to be His, He wants to take your spot on that old rugged cross, He doesn't want you to go to hell and suffer for eternity, He made you, He wants you to be His and no one else's. He desires to be yours, He is waiting with arms wide open. All you need to do is believe on Him "and how shalt be saved". "For with the heart man believeth unto righteousness; and with the mouth confession is made unto salvation". Romans 10:10.

Do you know why my parents are still together today? It is because of Jesus Christ. Most people when they go through a trauma such as mine and my brother's they pull apart rather than pull together and stick it out to the end.

My desire for this book is not for my glory, but to tell you that even at 5 years-old, when I went through that much trauma and trials in my life and kept going, that you can too. Now it hasn't been easy for me since that day, but God did it for a reason, I believe with all my heart that He did it to humble me and make me into what I am today.

To be a help to people, even though I have one good hand, I figure things out differently than other people do. I have learned how to do things with only one hand, when it takes two hands to operate, I just figure things out.

I believe too that God made me this way to encourage, to push you to "your" limits and "your" desires in life.

To be there if you need any encouragement, to help you succeed in life. I want to be a light to those around me in any way possible.

Love life to the fullest, be a help to those around you and you will be blessed by it. Just the joy that it gives me when I help someone out and don't expect anything back is priceless. So give of yourself and you will be blessed.

I believe too that God made me this way to be an example to those who think life is not worth living, to those who are crippled (because I used to be crippled), and I used to have the same difficulties and hard times, but through all of the difficulty in my life, with my parents behind me pushing me, saying come on Nathan get down there and crawl and do your exercises, they would drive me to the physical therapist every week and I would have to crawl on my stomach and then crawl and they would give me other things to do at home, and it was not easy, I struggled through it but my passion and my desire is to see you rise above your difficulties and fight with everything in you. To succeed and be truly blessed by God, who gave you the breath you breathe and the strength and the willpower to go after it. To stay focused on what is in front of you even though things may set you back in life, but you keep after it and you will succeed in life and God will bless you as well. Life is too big not to try, not to move forward, because when we fail, it should excite us to start right back up again and go after it again and again, to push and push until you win, can I tell you something, IT IS WORTH LIVING!!!!!

About the Author

Nathan Jirovec was involved in a horrific automobile accident at age five. He suffered massive head trauma that led to a long hospitalization and years of painful therapy.

Medical experts gave Nathan and his parents very little hope that their son would ever be able to live a normal life.

Ever speaking or walking normally was not in the cards for Nathan. But he was tenacious and unsinkable. He learned, through much pain and much work, to speak and walk. The damage to his brain permanently disabled one arm.

Nathan's family refused to treat him differently than their other children. Nathan refused to treat himself differently. He pushed himself and did not accept the limitations his body forced on him.

Nathan began a lawn business that grew into operating monstrous harvest equipment in rural Oregon and Texas. Nathan enrolled himself in college. Today he is a

ABOUT THE AUTHOR

college educated entrepreneur and engaged to be married.

Nathan Jirovec has accepted and overcome challenges most of will never face. Defeat and limitation are not in his lexicon and he has redefined "normal."

Today Nathan shares his inspirational story with groups of all sizes and ages.

Learn more about Nathan at www.findingnathan.com and connect with him on Facebook at https://www.facebook.com/nathan.jirovec.